Learning
to *Untie*
God's Hands

Learning
to *Untie*
God's Hands

Sherry York

Inspiring Voices®
A Service of **Guideposts**

Inspiring Voices books may be ordered through booksellers or by contacting:

Inspiring Voices
1663 Liberty Drive
Bloomington, IN 47403
www.inspiringvoices.com
1-(866) 697-5313

ISBN: 978-1-4624-0518-3 (sc)
ISBN: 978-1-4624-0519-0 (e)

Library of Congress Control Number: 2013901357

Printed in the United States of America

Inspiring Voices rev. date: 1/29/2013

To my husband, Tom.
Thank you for your support and the faith
that you have shown in me.
Thank you for believing
God had His hand on me.

Preface

On January 12, 2012, while driving home, I was talking to the Lord about writing a chapter for a book I had been asked to be a part of. I had never thought about writing until then. I did not have peace about it, so, after telling the Lord, *Okay, I'm not going to do it,* He began to flood my soul. In a matter of minutes I felt God had let me know I would write and have this title: *Learning to Untie God's Hands.* I was so excited. I texted my sister, who I thought would help me do this, and locked the message in my phone. But God let me know that I could do this with Him helping me. I began to write. I was amazed at what He gave me: a message of hope and help that so many are in need of. I'm so glad God has allowed me to be His instrument.

Acknowledgments

Thank you …

… my family,
without you I could never have done this.

… my sister, Dalina,
for all of your help in getting
this ready to publish.

… Nesmith Church,
for all your love and prayers.

… my wonderful friends
for all the encouragement.

Table of Contents

Introduction

The meaning of the word *untie* is "to unfasten or unloose; to free from a restraint or bond." We do not know how important it is to have full access to God. Without confidence in who we are in Christ, we cannot expect anything from God. God cannot go against His own Word. Hebrews 4:16 (King James Version) says,

> Let us therefore come boldly to the throne of grace, that we may obtain mercy, and find grace to help in time of need.

We should come to God with a clear conscience and a forgiving heart. Nothing can be in our way to the throne. To love God and to love your neighbor are the two greatest commands given by Jesus. If we fulfill these, we cannot break any of the others. It is impossible.

Our fall in America started with this: we want it our way, and we tied God's hands while turning loose Satan's. We can't change the world, but we can change ourselves and the church. In the following steps, I hope and pray that you hear from God, listen to Him, and untie His hands in your life.

Step One:
You Must Be Born Again

In order to untie God's hands, you must first be *in* God's hands. The most important step in untying God's hands is *you must be born again* (John 3:3 KJV). For most Christians this is not foreign, but sadly I believe that for some, it is. The church has made salvation not about true transformation. We believe Jesus died on the cross for our sins, for this is the truth. But we do not hear *you must be born again* very often. The Word says, "Except a man be born again, he cannot see the Kingdom of God" (John 3:3 KJV). To be born again means *to be made new*. To truly be born again, washed in the blood of the Lamb, is a transformation that can hardly be explained. But I want to share with you the moment I became a born-again Christian.

In the latter part of 1990, I was twenty years old and had been married for a short time to a non-Christian. It was about the time that the Gulf War began. The news of this scared me, because I had been raised by a true Christian mother who had taught us the Word of God. I remember calling her and asking her if this was the fulfilling of the end-times.

I wrestled with God for what seemed like months. One day, as I was wrestling with Him, I went to my bedroom to kneel down. But as I got one knee down, I said, "I can't, God. Not now." Satan was messing with my mind, telling me how things would change. He was making me worry about how this change would affect areas in my life—remember that I hadn't been married long. Satan does this every time he makes you feel like you will lose someone or something if you choose to be saved. He knew exactly what things to use to make me afraid.

Of all the things I had tried as a teenager, smoking cigarettes was the one thing that I loved doing, but I had always thought that if I was a Christian, I wouldn't want to. So to me, smoking would have to be given up. I thought about smoking just as drug addicts and alcoholics think about their addictions when God is calling them. I had also received a Bible as a Christmas gift, and I began to read it. When I read about Jesus dying for me, I thought, *I didn't ask Him to do it.* I didn't want to think I owed Him anything.

On January 13, 1991, I had been invited to church in Houston, Alabama. I remember smoking on the way there and telling myself, "This might be the last cigarette I may ever smoke, because I might be saved today."

The preacher, Brother Morris Helton, preached, and the convicting power of the Holy Spirit dealt with me. A friend of mine, Lori, was sitting with me. I am sure she noticed what was going on, because she asked if I wanted her to go with me to the altar. I said, "Yes," because I was tired of fighting. I went to the altar and knelt down, but here is where so many go wrong. I was asking the Lord with my mouth to forgive me, but I didn't mean it with my heart. I was still wrestling with the Lord. I was asking myself, "Do you really want to do this?"

My mother had always taught us and showed us that being saved was a serious thing. She knew that we would reach an age of accountability. I got up and sat on the altar bench. This was between God and me, and I knew it.

Jesus told that some people wanting to follow Him to "count the cost" before doing so,(Luke 26:33) and without knowing it, I was. I knew that I was at my crossroad when God spoke plainly to me: "If you leave here today, you will die. I won't deal with you anymore." I understand now that that meant Satan had plans to kill me, and God needed me with Him so He could protect me. When I knelt that time, I don't recall all that I prayed for, but the blood fell. I truly repented and surrendered everything I knew to Him. When I stood up, I felt so light, so free, so forgiven, and so new! I remember looking at the congregation and saying, "I can die now."

I had truly been born again and was given the free gift of the Holy Spirit.

The Bible talks of being born again as all things made new, and it was for me. I remember leaving the church that day. The sky looked new to me. I felt new. I had also made Satan very mad, because he once again had lost another to Jesus.

That evening, the church was having a baptism at the lake. I was on my way there, because I was one of the people to be baptized, and it was as if Satan was in the truck with me. I couldn't see him, but I could hear him. I felt like he was after me. I felt his anger. Yes, people, Satan is real just like God, and you better get ready to battle if you are a born-again Christian. Satan didn't want me to be baptized, which is why the fear was there. He wanted me to turn around, go home, and not serve the Lord. He wanted me to fear that being a Christian was too hard, and this fear is what I would have to endure. This happens to many people when they get saved. They never get rooted and grounded in the Lord because of it.

I thank God I did not give over to my fear. I feared God and an eternity in hell more.

After that day, I never smoked another cigarette. I had been completely delivered, and I have not ever desired it again. Jesus said, "If the Son therefore shall make you free, ye shall be free indeed" (John 8:36 KJV). I truly believe that when you surrender all to the Lord, He is more than happy to help you get rid of the junk that is holding you down. At forty-one years of age today, I know why I did not need to smoke: my lungs could not have held up to the smoke. I know this because now, chemicals such as bleach cause me problems. I can't tolerate smoke or any chemicals. There is no telling what would have happened to my health had I kept smoking. I thank God for setting me free and protecting me.

My born-again moment is not like everyone else's. I know this. But what I would like for you to take from this first step is a *know-so* salvation. I still make mistakes. We all do. We have to learn from them, turn from them, and move forward. Being born again does not mean that you are never going to make another mistake. It means you have an advocate with the Father who pleads your case, which is Jesus (1 John 2:1 KJV).

I believe that when you truly give your life to Him, you will not have to doubt it. Please understand that not everyone's salvation moment is like mine, or like yours. God has His own plan for each of us. We should all be sure of that moment when we were born again.

Step Two:
Untie God's Hands;
Read the Word

After you are born again, you are just a baby in the Lord. He holds us until we are a little older and more mature in Him. Then He gradually puts us down to take a step, just like parents hold their babies until they crawl. Eventually, you help them take their first steps.

As a new Christian, the most important thing you can do is read the Word. This is not what most new Christians are told today. But it is the most important thing you can do. It's the beginning of your relationship with your heavenly Father. This is how you will learn of Him and His ways. You will be able to see how real He is. It is how we become the best for our Father. God wants to give us the knowledge we will need on this journey through a life in Christ.

I encourage new Christians to read the New Testament first. We need to understand Christ and His wonderful love. The books in the New Testament tell us stories of great courage, faith, and happiness; even in the darkest hour, God never leaves His people. It is also full of great teaching to the New Testament Church—things to be aware of—and teaches us to have self-control. Yes, even though you are saved, God gives you a free will. Learning the Word will help you fight the enemy. Only through Jesus and the Word will you be able to fight the enemy and overcome the devil. It is sad to say, but I don't believe today's churches are teaching young Christians to study the Bible. They are led to believe as long as we meet three times a week everything will be fine. Meetings are not the problem. It is what we do with our time together that has become the problem. New Christians are not old enough in the Lord to recognize the voice of the devil nor studied enough to know what the Word says to throw at Satan when he is messing with their mind. I remember the devil doing everything he could to get me to give up on the Lord. Unfortunately, a lot of new Christians do not have that instilled as I had. Someone who has not been raised to know God hasn't got a clue as to what he or she is giving up on. That is where we, the church, have to help new believers: phoning them, paying attention to signs that they are struggling. I'm so glad that when I was a new Christian, I could call someone older in the Lord and say, "Hey, I'm feeling like … help me."

In 2 Timothy 2:15 it is written, "Study to show thyself approved unto God, a workman that needeth not to be ashamed, rightly dividing the Word of truth" (KJV). Believers need to read, and if you are unable to read, get Bible tapes or CDs. Listen as much as possible. Memorize all you can. Try to absorb all you can. The Holy Spirit will bring the Word to you as you need it. It will surprise you how well the Spirit does its part when you do yours. We as believers need to pray and ask God for daily wisdom and understanding of His Word. We should also be aware that Satan knows the Word. He can twist it and make it seem to mean whatever he needs it to at that time. You should always go to a mature Christian and tell them what scripture you are troubled with. They can help you because they have been there themselves. The more you study the Word, the more you will see how to fight Satan with it. It is your doubled-edged sword (Hebrews 4:12). Reading of how Jesus withstood temptation from the devil will teach you how to know the Word as He did. Yes, Jesus gave us wonderful examples of how to overcome, but you must dig for yourself to get the good out of it. Don't let anyone tell you what is in the Word. Learn it for yourself. Many Christians are easily deceived, not knowing the Word. The Holy Spirit will lead us by bringing the Word to our remembrance as we need it. The right Word for the right time.

When we are not totally surrendered to God, it makes Satan's job easier. There is a race set before us, with the giant prize of eternal life with God the Father and Christ our Savior. Let us do all we can to run the race well. In Matthew 23:37, Jesus said, "Oh Jerusalem, Oh Jerusalem, how often I would have gathered you, as a hen doeth her chicks, but you wouldn't let me" (KJV). We have to allow God's help. He never forces Himself. I think of this scripture from time to time. I think Jesus still says this today in different situations, in different ways. "Oh my people, Oh my people, if only you would have sought me, I would have numbed your pain. I would have healed your broken heart. I would have delivered you, but you wouldn't let me." Through the good, the bad, and the ugly, God is there for us. Seek Him and you shall find Him. Start today by untying the hands of God while tying up Satan's by reading and obeying God's

Word. Obeying the Word is necessary to untie God's hands. We cannot serve two masters; you cannot have the world and have God too. It is not possible. *God cannot and will not go against His own word.*

I know exactly what happens when you are out of the Word and the will of the Father. I was in the church. I had been saved for about six years. After several different preachers, I was feeling blah and started to attend a Baptist church near my home. I enjoyed it. I know God used me there. I had always studied the Word. God showed me many things, and I was able to teach. I had the youth and I loved them so much. Those were some of the best times of my life. We all know sometimes things happen in life and we have to make decisions. After nine years in a bad marriage, God made a way of escape. I never doubted that God set me free.

Two years after that, I married my current husband, Tom, who I am very thankful for. The road that led me where I am today was a little rough. We sin and we fall short when we do not stay in the Word. The devil can use discouragement as much as anything to destroy your life, and he tried that with me. After years of being in the Word, I quit reading it. I felt like such a failure. How could God want me again? I went years without a steady church to meet with and with no Word. I let people and circumstances cause me to feel so beaten down and discouraged. But, even though I wasn't reading His Word or going to church meetings, I never wanted to go back to who I was before I was saved, and I didn't. One day I said, *Enough!* I knew what I had to do from that day on. I was still delivered and saved. God had not given up on me and I hadn't on Him. He simply let me stay in that state of mind until I was sick of being sick, and from that day on, I was headed back to being in God's will and His Word. What I have experienced with God since then I never thought would be possible. You can do the same thing in your own life by not allowing the devil to hinder you anymore. God is a God of second chances, and as many as are needed to protect those He has called. For years, I had tied up God's hands and unloosed Satan's, giving him access to me that I didn't even realize. You can do the same thing that I did. Living and reading the Word of God will keep you from making so many mistakes. I wish I had never done anything out of God's will. What I learned from my mistakes is that God loves me more than anything and it doesn't matter what you think of me. It only matters what God thinks of me. Those words spoken to me the day of my made up mind will forever be one of the best revelations I've ever had. Church, let's get busy untying God's hands.

Step Three:
Untie God's Hands with Forgiveness and Prayer for Your Enemies

Being humble and forgiving are the two most crucial things in untying God's hands. I believe for the lost or saved, forgiving is one of the hardest things to do. It's so easy for us to feel justified when we feel like we or someone we love has been wronged. To be humble and to forgive go hand in hand. To start, one must humble himself before the Lord to get to a place where he can forgive. When we humble ourselves before the Lord, He can then give us direction in our lives. People may think that they are really getting close to God and then He starts getting closer too. That is when He begins to show what needs to be fixed and changed. It doesn't even matter if you feel justified. I remember having to fix some things in my life on my way back to being in God's perfect will. His will requires obedience.

It was the fall of 2009. I was working on my relationship with my Father. Being in God's Word, He began to speak to me through it. He let me know there were some things I needed to fix. The closer and more mature you get in the Lord, the more He will start perfecting you for His kingdom. That perfection doesn't come from human abilities of being what we think is perfect. It doesn't mean perfect in every way. It means perfect in God's love, God's unconditional love. The devil wants us to believe that it is impossible for God to love that way, much less for us to love that way too. It is only possible when you humble yourself, listen, and obey. I knew I had to. Sometimes, our mouth gets us into trouble, and sometimes making a bad decision that hurts someone else does. I had done both, and God the Father let me know I had to fix it. I wrote a letter to one person and sent some "I'm sorry" cards to another and her family. I had, not willingly, made some people mad at me, and I had to make this right in order to receive what God had in store for me. I never imagined what that would do. It turned God loose and tied up an area Satan no longer had control of. You see it didn't matter how the people upset with me responded; it mattered that I obeyed God. Freedom was found in obeying the Lord. You do your part and He will do His. He loves us so much. He wants to show us the capabilities we have through obeying His Word. It was worth fixing and mending those relationships because I want to love others and live a peaceful life. I never dreamed how God could love through me. When we humble ourselves before Him, we can see people the way He sees them.

There is power in forgiving, and it is so vital as a Christian to walk in that power. We are to imitate our Father in heaven. One night I was having a dream. I will not go into details, but just before I awoke these were the words

I was saying: "If I don't get up every day and show what God has done for me, how will they know what He can do for them?" I knew this was a message straight from God. To me it was powerful. We, the church, have forgotten what we are doing here. Lost people see us not forgiving and say, "Is that God?"

Paul tells the church to imitate him as he imitates Christ (1 Cor. 11:1 KJV). We all know Christ imitated the Father while He walked the earth. We are to walk the earth as citizens of heaven. Where have we gone wrong? We have tied the Father's hands by not humbling ourselves and by having an unforgiving attitude and spirit. The lost are watching us, and what are we showing them? We the church must start holding ourselves accountable to God's Holy Word. God wants us at our best; after all, we are representing the heavenly family. Being unforgiving will absolutely hinder your prayers. God can't go against His own Word. Jesus died for our sins. He gave us all a wonderful hope and an example of forgiveness to follow. Think of what doors would be opened with this one thing, forgiveness. I do not want to walk in non-forgiveness. I want to walk in the ways of the Lord and peace.

In the Lord's Prayer you recite the following words, "Forgive me as I forgive those who have sinned against me." In Matthew 18:21, Peter asked Jesus, "How many times should I forgive someone who has sinned against me? Seven times?" Jesus replied, "No not seven times, but seventy times seven" (KJV). We as Christians are to forgive our brothers and sisters in Christ, as many times as they ask us to. The Lord shows mercy to those who show mercy. Satan has lied to the world and to believers, telling them they have a right to feel the way they do, that they are justified. However, we as Christians surrendered that right when we accepted Christ and became new in Christ, just as Jesus gave up all of His rights when He died on the cross for our sins.

Actually, I decided to add *pray for your enemies* along with *forgiveness* after I had already written this book. I did not think about this being a part of the book until one day, on a Saturday, I was reading, going over my material for this book, and the devil began messing with my mind. I began to get a negative attitude making me feel like, *Why and what are you doing? No one is going to get it.* I felt sad and discouraged. I prayed that God would help me, wanting Him to encourage me in what I was doing. The next morning, my sister Dalina called me and I could tell she had been crying. She began to tell me God had given her another step for me to add to my book. Untie God's hands by praying for your enemies. When I hung up the phone, what I had read and posted days before on the computer hit me. God had answered my prayer and had given confirmation of what I should do. It was not at all what I expected but what we are all in need of. This is another way to untie God's hands and receive from Him what He has for us. Not only do we forgive our enemies, but we pray for them too. The Bible is full of stories about dealing with enemies and how God would like for us to handle them. There are some who go by the law of an eye for an eye and a tooth for a tooth. But even in the Old Testament, God was in control and expected those who were called by Him to handle things in His way. "Dearly beloved, avenge not yourselves … Vengeance is mine; I will repay, saith the Lord" (Rom. 12:19 KJV). Why Him? Because He is perfect and sinless. We are not. He is the creator of all, the great I Am. His thoughts are not our thoughts and His ways are not our ways (Isa. 55:8 KJV). We are in need of the same hope and mercy as our enemies. This is a real test in imitating God our Father.

Jesus said in Luke 6:27–38 (KJV),

> But I say unto you which hear, love
> your enemies, and do good to them

which hate you. Bless them that curse you and pray for them which despitefully use you. And to him that smiteth thee on the one cheek offer also the other; and to him that taketh away thy cloak forbid not to take thy coat also. Give to every man that asketh of thee and of him that taketh away thy goods ask them not again. And as ye would that men should do to you, do ye also to them. For if ye love them that love you, what thank have ye? For sinners also do even the same. And if ye lend to them of whom ye hope to receive, what have ye? For sinners also lend to sinners to receive as much again. But love your enemies, and do good, and lend, hoping for nothing again; and your reward shall be great, and ye shall be the children of the Highest; for He is kind unto

the unthankful and the evil. Be ye
therefore merciful, as your Father
also is merciful. Judge not and ye
shall not be judged; condemn not
and ye shall not be condemned;
forgive and ye shall be forgiven.

And in Proverbs 24:17–18 (New Living
Translation)

Don't rejoice when your enemies fall;
don't be happy when they stumble.
For the Lord will be displeased with
you and will turn His anger away
from them.

Job was being condemned by his friends,
saying these bad things must have happened
to him because of some sin he must have
committed. God's wrath was kindled against
his friends for not "speaking the thing that is
right" (Job 42:7 KJV). Job prayed for his friends:

"And the Lord turned the captivity of Job when he prayed for his friends …" (Job 42:10)

Satan hates relationships. God loves relationships. That is why He created it. God meant for us to need each other. Remember that God is love; and what is love? "Love is patient and kind. Love is not jealous or boastful or proud or rude. It does not demand its own way. It is not irritable, and it keeps no record of being done wrong … endures through every circumstance" (1 Cor. 13:4–7 NLT).

When we pray for our enemies, this makes us a little more like Christ. Praying for our enemies will lead to our prayers being answered and our bodies being healed. If you want to unloose the blessings and healings of God, then start today by forgiving and praying for your enemies.

Step Four:
Untie God's Hands by Getting Rid of Bitterness

It is written in Ephesians 4:31 to get rid of all bitterness, rage, anger, harsh words, and slander (NLT), as well as all types of evil behavior. Instead, be kind to one another, be tenderhearted, and forgive one another, just as God through Christ has forgiven you. Wow! What a mouthful and how hard to take in, especially in a world that says, "I have the right." It goes on to say in" Ephesians 5:1–2 "Imitate God, therefore, in everything you do, because you are His dear children. Live a life filled with love, following the example of Christ (NLT). The church this day and time has blown it, hasn't it? But, praise God! There is hope! Satan wants the church to lie down and die, but the Lord is saying, "Wake up! Untie me and allow me to work My power in your life." Now, in these last days, we need to untie God's hands in our own lives more than ever.

I had to let God show me His power in the area of bitterness in my own life. Bitterness leads to anger, rage, harsh words, and slander. Just being married is a test, a good test. Isn't it? When my current husband and I married, we didn't have much. He is a carpenter and I clean houses (which I love because it fits around my schedule for raising children). We have four boys; two of which are ours together. It is easy to overlook and not appreciate one another in a marriage. It is also easy for one to begin to think, *I do more and put more effort in this marriage than you.* Which in time will cause one to become bitter and filled with resentment. Bitterness and resentment can destroy your life and your home. I think marriage is a relationship the devil has a field day with. The devil hates relationship and he hates you. So he wants nothing more than for you to get mad and bitter over things that can be fixed. I had let him cause me to get this way simply because I did not know how to tell Tom what I was feeling, so I held it in. Tom could see the feelings on my face but he could not help that I was not willing to discuss them. For years, it changed my always-smiling face to a constant frown. Tom knew I was unhappy but he could not fix it. I thought I had the right to be bitter and angry, but I didn't.

After years of handling things my way, God spoke to me one day. He told me, "It is not Tom's fault. It is yours." God let me know that Tom had always been honest about what he could give and that I hadn't been about what I wanted. Tom was not responsible for my behavior; I was. That was a wake-up for me. I had to stop blaming Tom, who is still today an honest, good-hearted man. I didn't argue with God. I agreed. One day while Tom and I were in the kitchen, I was looking out the door and he was sitting at the table. I told him it was my fault and I was not going to blame him anymore. I had to make up my mind to let it go. The devil wanted me to remain quiet and stay mad on the inside rather than get it out and fix the problem.

From that day on, my marriage got better and better. Today, Tom and I are a team. We work, help each other, and have respect for what both of us contribute to our family. Not long after I allowed God to help me, I bought Tom a new wedding band and put it on his finger with a heart full of love instead of bitterness. God wants to give us a good life. Satan wants to steal it, destroy it, and kill it. There are marriages and people all over the world wasting away because of being bitter over something that is fixable with the help of our heavenly Father.

As long as I remained bitter, God's hands were tied and Satan's were loose. He was on my shoulder pointing out all the negatives and I was listening. God set me free, not only for the sake of my marriage, but also for the kingdom's sake.

I learned that nothing is worth losing heaven over. I love my heavenly Father for so many reasons. As a child of God, I am so thankful for His correction and His forgiveness. Turning Gods hands loose in my life has amazed me. I recognize Satan's traps and snares more quickly.

In October of 2011, I wanted my sweet ladies from church to come over to my home. I had prepared much for their coming. I love these ladies. I didn't want them over just for a visit. I wanted God to give me a word from Him to share and encourage them with. I started walking around the rug in my living room, praying and asking God, letting Him know this visit was about Him. He began to tell me, "Don't let the devil take you by surprise." We must be so close to Him that we recognize Satan's schemes. Powerful! I have to believe God planted a seed in their hearts and that they left knowing something God would later use for His glory.

Since that meeting, the devil has been busy. He has surprised us by destroying marriages and causing sickness. Many of us are still serving God with a smile on our faces and with a humble, dependent-upon-God attitude. Letting yourself get mad and bitter leads to wrong behavior. This allows Satan to enter our lives because we just invited him. Learn the Word. Recognize Satan's schemes and stop him in his tracks. The more you fight him through the Word, the less hold Satan will have on your life. Satan will try to use marriage problems, job problems, sickness and death to turn God's people away from Him. Understand that God has a plan. Don't try to figure it out. Trust Him. If Satan has made you bitter, he is stealing from you. Don't let him do this anymore! Turn it loose and allow God to show you how to heal. You are no good to yourself or anyone else if you continue to allow bad behavior to dominate your life. God wants you to allow Him to turn bitterness into sweetness.

Step Five:
Untie God's Hands
by Getting
Rid of Self-Pity

Self-pity is another thing that will tie God's hands. Jesus commanded us to love God and our neighbor. When you are in self-pity, it is easy to break these two commandments (which Jesus stated as being the most important) Matt 22:37-40. Satan sits on the shoulders of people every day and tells them they're pitiful. Unfortunately, he has destroyed many with this lie—for some, to the point of taking their own life. It is so sad to see hope for a person and for him or her to not see it for his or herself. I've seen people let self-pity destroy what they could be in Christ. Yes, Christians who have allowed self-pity to destroy them. Notice the key word here, *allowed*. We let Satan destroy us! It is only when we stop letting him control our behavior that things will change. You have to say, "No more, devil!"

Satan doesn't make you pitiful all at once. He does it gradually. So often we deal with marriage, raising children, and just everyday life and we forget to ask God how to do it. God wants nothing more than to tell us how but we have to ask. First, we have to understand that we have no control over others, only ourselves. We have to pray for others to do what they need to, and we should do what we need to. God never forces His will on anyone. He gave us free choice. With that choice, we can sit and do nothing, or we can get up and make a difference. If you can't do anything about your troubles or situation, then find someone you can help with his or her troubles. God will be working on your end for you because you're about your Father's business, which is to love and serve others.

People who live in self-pity can't help others. Ecclesiastes 3 says, "There is a time and a season for everything, even a time to weep." A time.

Not all the time. Oh, Satan would like for you
to. Can you imagine a world in which everyone
stayed pitiful? God help us if that were the case,
and thank God there are many who refuse to
stay there. Most with self-pity have so much
to offer other people, but they have listened
to Satan's lies and have chosen to believe him.
Satan has caused many to turn away from God,
from those they love, and from those who love
them because of self-pity.

Parenting is an area in which Satan can use
his weapon of self-pity. Mothers and fathers
become destroyed when their children make
bad choices that alter the dreams they had for
their children. The parents then self-examine
and blame themselves for the decisions their
children have made. Then, they feel that in
order for God to help them, they must change.
Being overwhelmed with that much change
causes them to be bitter. We have to *want* godly
change for the right reasons, not just to get what
we want. You never get to enjoy results this

way. Letting self-pity go too far will lead to bad behavior. It will make you jealous, unforgiving, envious, bitter, and angry. It will make you blame others and resent those who seem happy and successful. No one person is problem-free and it is a good thing that Jesus did not get pitiful. He was always concerned with others till his last breath, and now sits at the Father's right hand still concerned and interceding for us.

Self-pity will make you wish that others felt like you did and you will begin to try and hurt others. When you do this you have just broken the two greatest commandments: love God and your neighbor. God cannot go against His Word. We will reap what we sow, whether good or evil. God expects us to keep ourselves in check with the Word. He cannot do anything in your life when you are pitiful. You cannot mature in the Lord that way. Pitifulness will lead to selfishness, and that will tie the knot around His hands. The only way to get rid of this behavior is to repent and tell Satan, *no more*! And when you have done that, ask those you have hurt to forgive you and start with a clean slate.

I had times of feeling sorry for myself and I stayed down a long time. I had to realize that I was the only one who could fix me or allow God to fix and work on me. When I started doing my part, He was there with His hands untied, ready to help me. I thank Him that He had showed me what to do, to make lemonade out of lemons. It takes going through the valley to figure out how to get through the next valley. In the valley is where Satan is weaving in and out, telling lies and making you doubt, and making you feel hopeless.

In life, there are going to be valleys. You may have a spouse who betrayed you, children who brought you shame, or maybe you are enduring consequences for your own bad choices. But, if you are a Christian, there is hope and a new start. He did it for me and He will do it for you!

Jesus walked this earth, took stripes for our healing, died for our sins, and then rose from the grave. He went to be with the Father to sit at His right hand and make intercession for us. We have got to get hold of the enemy and his schemes. Today, you can make a difference in your life or in someone else until the victory comes to you.

Get rid of the self-pity. It is so ugly. If this is the carnal-minded rope that has God's hands tied in your life, allow Him to help you untie it.

Step Six:
Untie God's Hands
by Getting Rid of Pride

Proverbs 6:16–19 lists six things God hates, and the seventh one is an abomination to Him: a proud look, a lying tongue, hands that shed innocent blood, a heart that deviseth wicked imaginations, feet that be swift in running to mischief, a false witness that speaketh lies, and he that soweth discord among the brethren (KJV). Well, once again I must say, "Oh me!" We see this going on in our world today, and it brings nothing but trouble. God hates sin because sin destroys lives. God loves people so much. He sent His only begotten Son to die for our sins, to make a way of escape for the judgment that is coming.

Pride is the sin I would like to address here. The whole world, including today's churches, are full of pride. I am talking about self-righteous Christians. They are so proud of who they are and what they have achieved. The prideful who say they do not have to change, forgive, or love. Pride vexes many types of people, the lost and saved. They think it is okay for sin to be in their lives. They put God on a shelf until they need Him. Heaven forbid that we are concerned for our brother or sister in Christ. Yet, we think we are on our way to an award. *Wake up church and repent*! The churches need to examine the book of Revelation to make sure that we do not fall in any of those categories. After all, we are being examined by the lost and what are we showing them? Jesus? Unconditional love? Forgiveness? Humility? I am afraid we have not done a very good job considering the fact that most lost people cannot recognize the difference between Christians and themselves.

A lot of churches have allowed the pride of life to creep right in. In James chapter 2:1-4(NLT) the question is asked, "How can you claim to have faith in our Lord Jesus Christ, if you favor some people over others?" For example, suppose someone comes into your meeting dressed in fancy clothes and expensive jewelry and another comes in who is poor and dressed in dirty clothes. If you give special attention and a good seat to the wealthier person, but you say to the poor person, "You can stand over there or else sit on the floor," well, does this discrimination show that your judgments are guided by evil motives? (NLT) It goes on to say, "Love your neighbor as yourself."(James 2:8 NLT). Prestige has crept into the churches today, even little country churches. I've sat back and watched people fall all over themselves for the attention of someone who they thought to be somebody. We have made church a place where successful, proud, and sinful people can go, and we will make you feel all warm and toasty inside. Yes, even overlook the sin in your life. We will even go as far as making you think that you are saved and ready to go just because of who you are.

After all, we need that ten percent we preach on you giving, and making you believe all is well with your giving soul. *Wake up church, wake up*! What happened to the truth being preached whether you were rich or poor? The Bible was written for the church to live by. The lost are lost until they are saved; then they will need the Bible. There is nothing wrong with being rich. There is something wrong with how well we love our riches and the position it gives us.

The love of money has crept into our churches. Some preachers have found a way of getting rich by making others feel as if they have to give in order to be righteous. A little old lady on a fixed income selling her golden ring because it is all she had to send, while the preacher is driving a Cadillac when a Ford would have been fine. Is there anything wrong with driving a Cadillac? No, there is not. But, it is wrong if you are preaching for wealthy gain. I'm sure it was as easy for her to give up the ring as it would be for him to give up the Cadillac. Paul teaches much on giving. I believe he wouldn't expect anything from the church that he wouldn't be willing to give himself. Paul tells the church to not put yourself in a bind by giving what you do not have (2 Cor. 8:12–13 NLT). That is who I believe God is. Paul imitated the Father. We are no longer under the law. In Acts 5:1-4,(NLT) the church willingly sold all they had and gave to each other as they needed it. A couple, named Ananias and Sapphira, sold a possession and kept back part of it and laid a portion of it at the disciples' feet. The problem was that they lied about it when asked. Peter told Ananias the property was yours to sell or not sell, as you wished. And after selling it, the money was also yours to give away. How could you do a thing like this? You weren't lying to us but to God. The point of this scripture is that we have a New Testament choice in giving. It is called from the heart and you will be judged for what is in your heart. Some of the preachers of today will not tell you that. If you give for the wrong reasons, you give in vain and you can't buy your way into heaven (1 Cor. 13: 1–3, KJV).

The pride of life and the lust of the eye, the devil is sitting on the mountain while you are in the valley saying, "Look what you can have." Don't believe his lies! Just as Jesus, by example, used the Word to show us a way out of temptation, you must study the Word as a child of God or the devil will walk all over you. There is a difference between being ashamed of the mistakes you have made and being too proud to admit it. People kill me when they try to act like something they are not, especially Christians. It is sad when Christians are too proud to say, "My marriage has failed," or, "My children have brought me shame," or, "Please help me pray." There is a difference between being ashamed, non-trusting, and being like, "Oh, let me tell you how great everything is." Most of the time, people already know that it is not. I'm here to tell you that you are unloosing Satan's hands on you and your family, when the pride of who you are means more than the deliverance of those needing it.

As parents, raising children by example, I've seen the effects of our attitude being reflected in our children. We will answer, as parents before the Lord, for the examples we have set for our children. I have seen children grow up into teens with the same arrogant pride that I saw in the parents. This tends to come out when they are dealing with other people or even God. Children raised by parents who do not forgive will have trouble themselves with not forgiving. Parents who are pitiful teach their children to be pitiful. "I am the victim. Poor me, poor you." Prideful parents raise prideful children. We must be thankful, not prideful. The next generation are the next parents, leaders, husbands, and wives. We have a responsibility to raise good and decent people. Satan wants nothing more than for Christians to fail in this area. It makes it easier and easier for him to carry more and more to hell with him. After all, this is his goal. God wants all to get to heaven and escape hell. Satan works to ensure that this does not happen. We have tied the Lord's hands by our behavior problems. This is why we are sick, have marriages that fail, alcohol and drug abuse, and the list goes on and on.

Humble yourself before the Lord and He will lift you up. Pride is a problem that will keep you from admitting you are wrong and will keep you from forgiving and asking God to forgive you. Remember the parable of the religious Pharisee. In Luke 18:10–15, two men went into the temple to pray. One was a Pharisee who said, "I fast twice in the week, I give tithes of all that I possess." The other was a publican, who stood far off, and would not lift up so much as his eyes unto heaven, but smote his breast, saying, "God be merciful to me a sinner" (KJV). Jesus said, "I tell you this man went down to his house justified rather than the other; for everyone that exalteth himself shall be abased and he that humbles himself shall be exalted."

I've seen this in the churches today. Congregations will make the sinner feel guilty while patting the prideful Pharisee on the back. This happens because the truth isn't preached like it used to be. Preachers now depend on preaching as a source of income and when you offend the Pharisee, he goes somewhere else and takes his tithes with him. The church has to wake up and preach the gospel no matter whom it offends. The true Christians will prepare themselves through the Word regardless. Don't miss what God can do for you when you swallow your pride and decide Satan isn't going to use you anymore for his purpose. Untie the Father's hands by humbling yourself and He will lift you up.

Step Seven:
Untie Him and
Praise Him

One thing we do not do enough of is praising our heavenly Father. We get so busy asking for what we need or want that we forget to say thank you. I think praise can come in many ways. Living the Word would be a great start, I'm sure. Often, we see a lot of praising in church service, but I wonder how much of this is done when no one is watching. I am a bashful person and when put on the spot, I don't like that kind of attention. I sing at church and teach. You would think that I would be over being bashful or insecure, but I still feel fear. There have been times that I felt like I wanted to run and hide before I sung before the congregation. But, I know that is what Satan would have me do, and I cannot give him any control. Singing is a beautiful way to praise the Lord. Especially when no one is looking, it doesn't matter if you cannot carry a tune, as long as it is from the heart. I never thought about how much any of that mattered to God until now. Sometimes, I get caught up in singing and I feel the presence of the Holy Spirit. It is a wonderful thing to feel the Holy Spirit. I had a dream one night that I was in a church and I felt the Spirit of the Lord coming into the church. It was so real! I stood up and shouted three times as I took three steps toward it. It was one of the most wonderful dreams I had ever had. I wish I could dream it every night. I felt like the Lord was coming to get me. I look so forward to the Lord coming to get me because I am tired of this world and I want my children safe in the arms of Jesus.

There is a song with the lyrics, "Take these shackles off my feet so I can dance, I just want to praise Him, I just want to praise Him." That is what happened to me. He forgave me, He set me free, and now I have got to praise Him. There is nothing like God's forgiveness. It is the greatest gift ever, and I want to give that same forgiveness and walk in it everyday. Thank you Jesus for saving my soul! Satan wants you to believe that God has given up on you and that He did let go. He did not let go. He is right where you left Him. Find Him again. Oh, the joy that awaits you when you find Him! I knew that I was nothing outside of Jesus and I still know it. He is my confidence, my comforter, provider, healer, and lover of my soul. For the first time ever, I now know that no one loves me like the Father. I hope and pray that someone will read this and start to find out how much God, our Father, loves him or her. Maybe that person is you. You see, if we can grasp this, Satan has lost the hold he has on our lives. Praising God will just happen before you know it.

I believe true praise from a child of God is what He values, not counterfeit praise. Yes, God does know the difference. Another form of praising that will get God's attention is to praise Him for things that have not came to pass yet. Believing the promises of God and trusting Him to do His part. He wants nothing more than for you to have good things according to His will for your life. God sometimes protects us by not giving us what we want because He knows it would not be good for us. For instance, some cannot be millionaires. It would ruin who they are in Christ. Some have to go through the learning points to be better for the Lord's work. God has a perfect plan for our lives and we have to trust Him. When the devil lays his snares, God will make a way of escape. If we miss and mess up, He will be there to dust us off and start again.

We can praise God for the good things that are coming. Believe that God is good and He can't be bad. And when bad comes, know that the devil has just shown up. Praise God anyway.

In July of 2004 my dad had to have open-heart surgery. He had six by-passes, one being the widow-maker artery. Anyone familiar with blocked arteries knows how serious that can be. Dad went from 2004 to 2009 without medicine before having trouble in the fall of 2009. Some arteries were blocked and they tried to use the balloon method, but it failed so they used a stint. My dad was not a Christian. He had never confessed that he had been born again. Although he did believe—he had the same preacher as the rest of the family: mother. I loved my dad very much. I knew he wasn't perfect and could have made a lot of better choices. I also believe my dad could have been used by God to do great things for the Lord. Witnessing to him was a little hard. I never really knew how to approach him and, as I said, I knew that he knew.

One day the Lord spoke to me after dad's heart problems rose up again. He let me know that my dad was going to die in November. I know this is hard to believe but it is true. I was so broken and began to pray and beg God for more time on daddy's part. I prayed for him to be saved. I could let him go if I knew heaven would be his home. But the thought of hell was more than I could bear and I grieved. I decided to write daddy a letter to witness to him so that I could say what I wanted. I also got him a copy of the sinner's prayer, framed it, and set it by his bed. I like the prayer because it read, "I know I can't save myself." Dad was always a strong manly-man and never wanted to show fear. He needed to know this was something he couldn't do on his own.

Thanksgiving Day the family was to get together at my parent's house. Dad just did not look good. He went to the living room and I went and sat with him, holding his hand as tears streamed down my face. We never spoke. I was just thinking on what I knew the Lord had shown me. The next day, dad had to go to the hospital. The doctor had already said there was nothing else he could do. This is why it is important to listen to God and pray. Daddy's doctor was off for the holiday and another doctor was on call. We laid hands on dad and prayed for him before going back to surgery and even then he never showed fear. When the doctor came back out to us, he told us the stint was already blocked 75 percent. All he could do was a stint inside of a stint. My heavenly Father let me know what was coming and offered me a chance to pray for him and ask God to show my earthly father mercy. The doctor told him he had to take the new medicine and never miss a day in order to live.

Daddy made it from that day until July. Two weeks before he died he had quit taking the medicine. He did not like the way it made him feel. The week before he died he went to revival with my oldest sister Vicki who had witnessed very boldly to daddy often. During that week mother said he would sit in the recliner and say, "I wish I could go back and do things different." That Saturday at my uncle's shop he had told someone who was cursing that he was trying to do better and that he should too.

Sunday evening on July 18th, I called dad to tell him I needed him to watch my youngest boy Caden (Dad was the best babysitter). He said he had been doing some work outside and had to come in because he wasn't feeling well. He said he wished that he had made a right instead of all of those lefts. My son and I both told him we loved him. I told him I would call mother to see how close she was to being home. She had to take our grandmother to a reunion that day and she was gone. It was about 5:00 p.m. when I had called him. Mother got there about 6:00 p.m. By 6:30 my dad had passed away. My praise in all of this is that regardless of what my dad chose to do, my heavenly Father answered my prayer and he showed my dad mercy and compassion. I have hope that daddy repented, and hope in God's mercy, just like the thief on the cross.

My mother had to go to the hospital for what she thought could be her heart around November or December of 2011. I panicked at first; I thought, *not mother*. But then the words from the ladies meeting at my house came back to me, "Don't let Satan take you by surprise." I started quoting scripture, "Oh death where is thy sting ..."1Corin 15:55(KJV). You see, mother is a child of God, and mother will be fine. I knew my mother would be okay if she lived or if she died. Praising God stopped the attack Satan had planned. There is no sting in death with Jesus. Whether we live or die, we are His.

In my prayer notebook, I have written not only my prayers, but my praises, and my thanks. I write down the things that are hurting me and I thank Him for healing me. God wants us to walk in good health but we must take care of our bodies. You do your part and He will do His. There is much to be thankful for. Look at your life. Write it down. This way, you will not even forget the simple things. If you really want to tie up Satan and set him in the corner where you have had God, learn to praise Him.

Closing

To whoever reads this, I hope and pray that God has revealed something to you that you have needed. He has helped me so much since I allowed Him to help me. I love you with God's love and pray you see God as He wants you to. He wants you to see that He loves you. He wants you to hear Him and follow Him. God showed me His love for people and now I look at people differently. He is our creator. We get excited when our children have blessed us. So does our heavenly Father when we bless Him. Our hearts break whenever we see our children on a wrong path, so does His when we choose a wrong path. If only all could see with His eyes and His ears. I also pray for godly wisdom and discernment. God wants us all to have the things we need to fight the enemy. In order to do that, we must imitate the Father and walk in His ways.

I had to learn God's ways through the Word and through listening to the Holy Spirit. This is how God showed me what to get rid of in my life. I have read the New Testament more times than I can count. Some years back, I went back through with my questions. I went back through studying tithing and what is the meaning of church. I believe God let me see some things that I had never noticed before. I, for the first time in my Christian life, seen what the temple is: we the body of Christ, and I understood the Law and our freedom from it. When I say this I mean freedom in Christ not freedom to sin.

Sin is bondage to Satan and I do not want any part with or of Satan. We as Christians have a responsibility to our temple and our church. New believers have to grow and learn from the milk of the Word, while older Christians need to be on the meat of the Word. The Word also tells us that the Holy Spirit will teach us the Word. I personally do not want to rely on a preacher to teach me God's Word. I want to know it for myself and let God teach me daily. Now that does not mean that we do not need preachers. We need all of God's workers working together for the Kingdom. But, we do need to know the Word for ourselves so that we will not be deceived. As we all know, not all preachers are of God, or some left God without telling anyone (meaning they are not living it but are still in the pulpit). It is so vital to have your own personal relationship with God. It is how He gets us to where we need to be in Him and His will. I cannot stress enough how you need to know your heavenly Father on a personal level so that you can be personal with Him. You need to tell Him everything, even when you think that it does not matter. Remember, it matters to Him.

I was at the local store one day in line checking out and behind me was a lady with a few food items in her cart. When I left the store my heart was broken because I thought, *Lord, is that all she could afford?* I know what that is like because I have been there myself. I felt the Lord say to me, "My heart breaks too." I hadn't thought about God thinking like that. Some would say, "Why doesn't He fix it?" I am here to tell you that that is why *we* are here. God put us here for each other. That was how God planned for things to be accomplished. We are supposed to imitate the Father. We are supposed to love each other and our enemies. You see, God lets it rain on the just and the unjust alike. We get good from God regardless of who we are or how we act. God can only be good. This is truth. Satan can only be bad. He is here to kill, steal, and destroy. God wants to give life, abundant life, through Jesus.

God has allowed me to go through these things because had I not, I would not be able to help others. I see things so differently now, so much better and more like my Father. I now have more compassion than ever for Christians who have fallen short. You see, walking a mile in another man's shoes will show you who you really are. I had to see myself as God was seeing me: the bitterness, non-forgiveness, discouragement, and hopelessness. All this equals bad behavior. I know what it is like to tie God's hands and be blind to it. I know what it is like to let Satan steal from you. I did it for years. There will be things never recovered from that time, but with my heart and eyes on Jesus, I will not let Satan steal anything else. Is this possible? I believe that it is only if you stay close to the Father. Hebrews 12:1–2 reads, "Therefore, since we are surrounded by such a huge crowd of witnesses to the life of faith, let us strip off every weight that slows us down, especially the sin that so easily trips us up. And let us run with endurance the race God had set before us. We do this by keeping our eyes on Jesus, the champion who initiates and perfects our faith" (NLT).

Keeping our eyes on Jesus, this is how we can keep God's hands free in our lives and recognize Satan before he can accomplish his plans. With the steps from this book that have helped me, I believe you will be amazed at what will happen in your own life if you apply these steps. Jesus is to return soon for a church that has prepared itself for His coming. In Revelation chapters 2-3 seven churches are told what to do in order to prepare. But even if His return is a long way off, death could still be at your door. The lost still need to know our Savior and our brothers and sisters in Christ need stable leadership. We are responsible for setting an example of our heavenly Father; not perfect in every way, but perfect in love, His love. There is a message to be preached right there within itself. The first two commandments sum it all up. Let us challenge each other and walk in our Father's ways. Let us untie the father's hands and let the blessings and healings begin, in Jesus' name. Amen.

About The Author

Sherry York is the wife of Tom York. Their children include Brett, Rhett, Colby, and Caden. They live in Addison, Alabama. Sherry loves being a mother to her boys, which she thought she would never have. She loves her job of serving others. She enjoys sharing God's Word and ministering to others in need when given the opportunity.

Sherry would love to hear from you if reading this book helped you in any way. Please e-mail her at tsyork@hughes.net or write:

Sherry York
643 County Road 130
Addison, Al 35540

Thank you and I pray God blesses you with His awesome wisdom; it is all you will ever need to succeed.

Sherry York